South African Mining Nationalization

South African Mining Nationalization

Abraham Mathebe

Library of Congress Control Number:		2010911800
ISBN:	Hardcover	978-1-4535-5761-7
	Softcover	978-1-4535-5760-0
	Ebook	978-1-4535-5762-4

This book was printed in the United States of America.

To order additional copies of this book, contact:
Xlibris Corporation
0-800-644-6988
www.xlibrispublishing.co.uk
orders@xlibrispublishing.co.uk
300639

PREFACE

To write and speak simply and yet comprehensively to the world about economic and wealth distribution factors in South Africa requires great skill and deep understanding of how wealth is currently distributed in the country, particularly in mining, as this book will dwell in a specific sector's wealth distribution.

This book is thus deliberating on South African mining debate on mines nationalization, which has attracted the attention of the investors, as the president of the country has vigorously reiterated the fact that the matter has not been in the policies of the ANC (the ruling party in SA). Since the matter is of a public interest, South Africans will preserve their democratic rights to raise their opinion in this matter. This will, however, be officially debated at the African National Congress conference that will be held in 2012.

We in South Africa are saddened by the rising cost of living. Inflation fluctuation continues to cause more pain and hardship than most people are able to bear. Unemployment is worse than ever. It is, therefore, imperative that our political leaders start to get out of their comfort zone and take into cognizance the fact that SA mines could play a pivotal role in changing the lives of the ordinary citizens of the country across the colour spectrum. However, this would happen only if the wealth is shared equitably.

As fascinating, every reader is encouraged to read this book to their utmost comprehension so they may have a clear understanding of the bases of what prompted the author to write this book in critics on South African mining and its true operational reflections.

This book does not have an index. It is because the writer fears that the readers will turn to the spots of their interest and read no further I therefore reiterate the importance of reading the entire book with a conscious mind which will assist you in getting the background of the book in its entirety just before applying your mind on the reflections of the book as captured by the author of the book.

The author will appreciate your comments.

Please send your comments to: *abrahammathebe@webmail.co.za*

Good luck!

By mine employee, Abraham Mathebe (South Africa)

NATIONALIZATION OF MINES IN SOUTH AFRICA: WHAT IMPACT WILL THAT BRING?

Kindly allow me to share with you the feeling of the ordinary employees working in South African mines across the country and relate this book to the debate that has been heading the news recently in SA on nationalization of mines.

I would like to give special thanks to Xlibris UK, for affording me this opportunity to have my *debut* book published under their mentorship as experts in the industry thereof. I particularly give special thanks to and appreciate the manner in which Mae Gibbs of Xlibris welcomed and introduced me to the rest of the team at Xlibris.

I, therefore give thumbs up to the mineworkers for reviving a debate on the nationalization of mines in South Africa. You would therefore allow me to reflect as far back in 1990 when *Bobby Godsell* was interviewed by *Learn and Teach* about issues of privatization and nationalization.

Should I not include the philosophy of other leaders and officials who have previously deliberated on the crux of the matter of this topic, my comment would indeed be naïve . . .

Bobby Godsell was described as a 'man with many portfolios.' He was a director of Anglo American Corporation's industrial relations and public affairs, office of the chairman, and chairperson of the manpower committee of the South African chamber of commerce. He held the portfolio of labour legislation of the South African employers' consultative committee on labour affairs. He served on the economic advisory council of the state president in that time and was the vice-president of chamber of mines, and eventually ended in *Eskom*.

I just ask myself how Bobby Godsell managed to run all these offices efficiently. Allow me to get down to the nitty-gritty of the article.

The following were questions deliberated to the man with many portfolios by *Learn and Teach*.

Q. Perhaps, we can start off by asking you if your view is that of the majority of people in the private sector.

Godsell: Firstly, let me say that the private sector is not a movement. It is really the many thousands of businesses that are privately owned in the country. On many issues the people in the private sector do not agree. So I cannot say that I am speaking for the private sector as a whole. I can only give you the broad view of Anglo American. Anglo American has two goals – *firstly, to have an efficiently-run economy that we can create as much wealth as possible, and secondly, to have a fair distribution of wealth to all South Africans.*

In my view as an author of this letter, I find some words spoken by this man very ambiguous. I am referring to words such as *firstly we can create as much wealth as possible.* Mr Godsell could have meant something else but in my intellectual view this is construed to be self-explanatory in a sense that a man was showing the tenacity of self-enrichment collectively with his constituent assembly he represented as he stated unequivocally that he did not speak for the private sector as a whole; now as a reader, I believe that it is also within your prerogative to have a different interpretation. *But as for me, I write what I like, fearlessly.*

Mr Bobby went on and said: *secondly we need to have a fair distribution of wealth to all South Africans.* What do you think he could have meant? Come on reader, open your mind! Mr Godsell was parabolically entrenching the barriers of *us and them.* His sentence alluded to the assertion of creating as much wealth as possible for themselves and the South Africans in the later stage. This practice has increased job losses to 25.2% in South Africa.

In my research, Mr Godsell was also recorded to have said: 'The question of whether or not we nationalize or privatize is a relevant one, but the real question is how we can best achieve the creation of wealth and its fair distribution. This is what all South Africans should be asking themselves.' Nationalization and privatization are not goals but the means of achieving the goals.

Apart from the ambiguity Mr Godsell has shown, I find this to be of paramount importance, which suggests that we as a country need to focus on how we successfully distribute wealth throughout the country and its dwellers.

I do not wish to miss an opportunity in taking you further to some of the questions asked to Mr Bobby Godsell.

Q. It is well known that you are in favour of privatization. Do you support the privatization of all state corporations?

Godsell: I support privatization because I believe that the private sector runs businesses more efficiently and productively. However, I also believe that there are businesses that should be nationalized. Businesses that can be nationalized are *natural monopolies* such as police and Eskom.

Now, in this deliberation, Godsell gave examples of businesses that he believed should be nationalized.

As I was preparing for this book, I was still shocked with dismay to learn that Godsell never bothered to give his opinion about mining as much as he did in mentioning other operations which in his view should remain nationalized, given the fact of the mining set up, there is unequivocal monopoly in mining sector, I could not understand the reason why Mr. Godsell decided to keep his opinion on this sector, could it be the reason that he was also benefiting from the operations as one of the bosses in chamber of mines? The answer in a clear YES! He further stated: 'One should not undermine people's right to choose. I went to the German Democratic Republic, East Germany, a few years ago. There was no inflation and the health services were good. But the people decided not to vote for the communist party in the recent elections. One of the reasons was because they wanted to have choices which they did not have under forty years of communist rule.'

Mr Godsell has been parabolic again. This statement is simply saying that politicians must understand that it is about the people's choice and not the individual's and the capitalist's choice. Indeed, this would not have come out of Mr Godsell's mouth; it is true that South Africa and its wealth must belong to the people of the country, and let the people make their own choices about wealth distribution even in a mining sector. Godsell would not have been straightforward in his statement as he could have vetoed his ideology of accumulating wealth.

He further advised that public-owned companies should have a board on which representatives of the state, the employees, and the public will sit. In this way, all the relevant interests will be represented.

Without wasting your precious time, let's read about how Floyd Mashele answered the questions asked by *Learn and Teach* in 1990 about nationalization vs privatization.

Floyd Mashele was the second national vice-president of Post Office and Telegraph Workers Association known as POTWA, and he was also on the union's campaign committee. In addition, he was the national coordinator of COSATU'S anti-privatization committee.

Q. What is COSATU'S view of South Africa's future economic policies?

Floyd: We are looking forward to a mixed economy in which the public sector, the private sector, and the cooperatives will have a role to play.

Q. It is well known that COSATU supports nationalization and is against privatization. Can you tell us why COSATU supports nationalization?

Floyd: First of all, I should repeat that we want a mixed economy. We are not talking about nationalizing every business or corporation, only the *big state-run corporations*. We support nationalization because we believe that these corporations can help the new government deal with inequalities and provide services at a low and reasonable rate.

In my view, in the event where Floyd mentioned *big state-run corporations* he could have also referred to businesses such as Eskom, Iscor, mining etc.

Floyd is now flowing. 'In this country, black people have been disadvantaged for over three hundred years [remember that it was November 1990 when this was recorded]. The little land we had was taken over by force and by laws such as the 1913 Land Act. Black people earn low salaries. They do not have enough education or skills. The rate of unemployment among blacks is very high,' said Floyd. 'About seven million people live in shacks in the Pretoria, Witwatersrand, and Vereeniging area alone,' he added.

'In the short term we need to create 4,50,000 jobs a year. If we are to keep with the population explosion, we need at least 8,50,000 houses in the black areas, and several schools, hospitals, crèches, roads, and so on. To create those jobs, schools, hospitals, and so on, the state needs the resources that big nationalized corporations can bring. The trade union movement is prepared to look at other ways of getting resources. *If there is any other effective way, let us have it.*'

Q. What do you say to the argument that nationalized industries are inefficient and unproductive?

Floyd: The government's concern has never been to run them efficiently [referred to the government of the National Party in South Africa which was in power for over 40 years prior 1994] in a business-like manner. They ARE run according to apartheid principles of giving jobs to *arm en ongeleerde boere* [poor and uneducated Afrikaners].

We are not convinced that enough has been done to make these services run efficiently and productively. We should be looking at how we can make nationalized corporations efficient instead of just saying, 'It cannot work!'

Q. The Soviet Union and other Eastern European countries are said to be moving away from nationalization in a favour of privatization. Yet the labour movement in South Africa wants to nationalize.

Floyd: We can only learn from what happened in other countries and be wise enough not to commit the same mistakes.

What happened in the Eastern Europe and Soviet Union does not have direct influence on us. Conditions in those countries are different from ours and reasons for moving away from nationalization may not even be the same as the South African government's reasons.

We want to emphasize that nationalization in our country is aimed at giving resources to the state in order to be in a position *to deal with apartheid injustices.* The Soviet Union and other Eastern European countries did not have a system called apartheid.

I now hope that a reader has just read the whole thing between the lines, as we are coming back to the issue of our SA mines nationalization.

As an author, I do not understand why our leaders seem to be embroiled about making an informed decision about nationalizing our mines.

It will be inappropriate for some of us to suggest that the government cannot run this sector efficiently and profitably. We will definitely be prejudicing the whole thing without thinking wisely. It is not true that private companies are always efficient and profitable. For example, the telephone company in Britain called British Telecom was originally state-run. It was then sold to a private company. Soon after it was privatized the corporation became inefficient, and the British government had to intervene in order to make sure that services were provided.

Privatization has always been a calculated political strategy; its aim was to make sure that the government of today will not have any resources. This will mean that poverty and unemployment will remain relentless in the country and the poor people are taxed more money in the country. Many political leaders in South Africa are loosing the tune of *batho pele* (people first), defected from their original positions for the love of money and self-enrichment.

Our leaders are failing to underpin the essence of mining charter which insists that the minerals of the country be controlled by the people of the country. Some already own big shares in the mining sector when others are still on a waiting list. This is the only reason why they do not want to support mine nationalization.

Poor communities in South Africa are still impoverished and yet not immune to bank charges that every citizen in the country of South Africa is subjected to irrespective of their financial status [there is no exceptional treatment to the poorest of the poor in bank transaction charges, the amount millionaires pay for bank charges is the amount a poor South African pays].

This is the ordeal of a mineworker who was working for Western Platinum Mine in Rustenburg.

I work at Western Platinum Mine in Rustenburg. The problem is that we need someone to come and speak to the general manager, J. B. Macfarlane. We have so many complaints, but he would not listen to us. The first thing is that the wages we get are very little. The second thing is the dirty hostels we live in. Also the whites hit us at work especially at shaft no. 4. Please ask our leaders to come and help us.

Oppressed worker, Marikane.

As I was typing this cry-for-help article, I could not hold my tears running down my cheeks.

The minister of minerals and energy has in terms of section 100(1)(a) of the Minerals and Petroleum Resources Development Act, 2002 (Act 28 of 2002), developed the housing and living condition standards for the minerals industry, which has not been equitably adhered to in the mining sector.

The mining companies in consultation with other stakeholders shall assist financially and facilitate the acquisition of land within close proximity of the mine and plan their housing needs in support of compact, integrated, and mixed land use environment; the housing development must consider and be based on the integrated development plans (IDP's). In this publication, non-compliance with the housing and living conditions standard will render the entity to be in breach with the MPRDA and subjected to section 47 of the Act. This act has been promulgated in 2002 and did not bear any fruit for the lowly paid mineworkers.

I am a mineworker who knows how black people are being treated in this sector. As blacks we still need a diploma or a degree in order to get promotion, unlike our white counterparts who only have to write their names down which will be equivalent to a diploma or even a degree in order for them to qualify for a promotion. How long should blacks and whites remain foes in this industry? Our leaders are turning a blind eye to it. I may have been a bit young around the time when the late Chris Hani was murdered. But from what my brother Charles has been telling me about the love of Hani to his people as he worked very closely with him, I do not think that blacks would still be exploited as such and treated like animals in this sector if Hani was still alive today. Indeed, white people knew where it hurt the most by killing this man.

I sent an email at least twice to the federation's office (COSATU) in an attempt to finding out as to what the federation's standpoint on the issue of mine nationalization is. But it did not make any sense to them as they did not respond to it. I, however, do not wish to entertain a thought that crosses my mind suggesting that it is because I am just an ordinary mineworker who should not be asking such questions according to my comrades at COSATU. Contrary to that I am a mineworker who has generated billions of rands and dollars in this sector, which I did not benefit from.

I am confessing that this correspondence represents the views of all the oppressed mineworkers who are in support of South African mines nationalization.

**Understanding mining looking at the history,
which should help us determine the equitable
wealth distribution which Bobby Godsell alluded to.**

Large deposits of diamonds were found in the Kimberly area in 1867, over a hundred years ago. Blacks and whites flocked to the area from all over the country to dig up these precious stones. This was the beginning of a huge change to the South African economy and to its entire people's way of life. The economy would no longer be based on farming but on mining.

First, anyone could come and dig for diamonds, but as diamond-digging got deeper, water started seeping in, and pumping it out was difficult and expensive. Many small holders were forced out, and businesses with money started to take over the operations in diamond mining and made rules that stopped blacks from owning diamond claims. People like Cecil John Rhodes made fortunes from the diamond fields. Fifteen years later, all blacks were kicked out of mining claims and a few big capitalists controlled the richest diamond mines in Kimberly.

In the 1880s, the apartheid government working with the mine bosses brought in new systems and laws to control the movement of mine labour laws which miners suffered under for many years—a law that allowed the bosses to strip and search black workers to find stolen diamonds. Black workers were forced to wear mealie sacks so it was hard to hide diamonds. These laws were made to take power away from black mineworkers.

In 1884, Cecil John Rhodes set up De Beers, consolidated it, and got permission from the government to use unpaid prison labour on the diamond mines. Young black work seekers would be arrested for not carrying a pass, put in prison, and end up working on the diamond mines for no pay. De Beers used free prison labour until 1932. A historic Cullinan diamond mine was one of the De Beers' giant mines. The original 3.106 carat became the largest rough diamond ever discovered when it was found on 26 January 1905 by miner, Frederick Wells. Once polished, the stone was presented to King Edward VII and forms part of the British Crown jewels. Its value has been estimated to be in excess of 200 million pounds.

It was only overtaken by the world's biggest polished diamond in 1985 with the discovery of the golden jubilee diamond also at the Cullinan mine. That stone was smaller than the original on discovery but had a larger polished weight of 545 carats.

Cullinan mine has also produced several of the world's other largest diamonds including the famous centenary diamond at 599 carats rough under the new ownership.

Another law said that natives could not use the explosives in the mines. The blasting had to be done by more skilled and better-paid whites. All black workers had to be supervised by some white man as their master, so black people were taught to become inferior to whites in all mining activity. After gold was found in 1886 on the Witwatersrand (this is Afrikaans which in English means the ridge of white waters), government quickly put a law in place saying that Africans could not own gold mines.

I believe I have already elaborated more than adequately about South African history in mining in order for you as a reader to make an informed opinion about the issue of mines nationalization. *South African history is very interesting and yet so painful.*

I am only giving you a brief background on how wealth has been distributed in this sector since 1867. From 1987, National Union of Mineworkers (NUM) started fighting for the dismantling of the single-sex hostel accommodation system in mining which formed part of the migrant labour system of control. The NUM underpinned the democratic running and upgrading of hostels as a priority campaign in line with its policies of taking control of the hostels. The NUM has achieved so many things in protecting the dignity and human rights of the mineworkers. However, to this day we are still sitting with a problem of wealth distribution in this sector. Black workers still remain the lowly paid employees. Seventy per cent are still in stinking hostels without proper sanitation. These workers cannot afford shelters for their loved ones; thanks to the pittance they are getting paid.

Post-1994, South African government introduced the so-called Employment Equity Act (EEA), which was promulgated in a national legislature, and introduced to all sectors across the board. The intention of this act was to redress the previous imbalances of depriving blacks, Indians, and coloureds to participate in better paid positions. However, a weakness of this act has been the fact that there is a penalty in the form of a fine which is not more than 1,000,000 rands that the company would pay to the department of labour should they be found to be non-compliant to EE. Mining companies are generating millions of rands per hour, and this makes them feel no pain at all when they pay such fines due to their arrogance towards this act. Hence the employment equity act remains a phantom.

If we cannot speed up the process of redressing the previous imbalances, we will eventually find ourselves to be wanting. We cannot have the so-called Employment Equity Act, black business empowerment, and all other discriminatory programmes for eternity. There should be some time where such programmes are phased out. However, as long as we are still having a problem of unfair wealth distribution which results in the poor being more impoverished, we will still claim to have such programmes in action in trying to resolve and alleviate poverty amongst the previously disadvantaged communities. For now, such programmes are of greater importance.

I have been employed in mining for eight years now. I participated in work politics since I started working for the mine and have learnt how arrogant the employer can become in this sector. The employers have managed to bring down the force of our trade unions by showering our top leaders and their spouses with big birthday presents or even handshaking surprises. We have so many leaders with controversial clouds hanging on them at all times, following them wherever they go. In this sector in particular, you will find an old man who has been working for a particular mine for more than thirty-six years and still cannot afford a shelter. When you look at the clothes they are wearing, you will hardly believe that they are employed. You will see a toe protruding out of their shoes. If you ask why they cannot buy a new pair of shoes, the reason would be, 'I have five children, and two of them are at the college. Therefore, I choose to assist them because they should not end up where I am today.'

A detailed picture of the wages/salaries and categorization in this sector, especially in diamond mining.

These categories determine the salaries and wages according to their differences (from the lowest to the highest paid individuals).

- Category A2 = 100% black workers (this is the lowest-paid wage category)
- *(Wage gap from the lowest R2,800 per month)*
- Category A3 = 100% black workers (the second lowest-paid wage category)
- Category B1 = 100% black workers(the third lowest-paid wage category)
- Category B2 = 99% black workers (wage)
- Category B3 = 45% blacks and 55% whites with higher salaries than their black colleagues (whites earn salaries and blacks earn wages)
- Category B4 = 45% blacks and 55% whites with higher salaries (55% of whites from category B3 will still earn higher than 45% of blacks from category B4)
- Category C1 = 15% blacks and 85% whites with higher salaries (55% of whites from category B3 will still earn higher than 15% of blacks from category C1)
- Category C2 = 9% blacks, coloureds 1%, and 90% whites with higher salaries (some whites from category B3 still earn higher than blacks from C2)
- Category C3 = 3% blacks and 95% whites with higher salaries
- Category C4 = 2% blacks, 1% coloureds, 1% Indians, and 96% whites with higher salaries

- Category D1 = 1% blacks and 99% whites with higher salaries (98% whites from C4 earn higher than blacks from D1 category)
- Category D2 = 100% whites (first management level)
- Category D3 = 100% whites (high management level)
- Category D4 = 100% whites (higher management level)
- Category EXCO = 100% whites (highest decision making body in the operation) *(Wage gap to the highest +—R300,000 per month)*

The following is how a partisan grading is used in most of the diamond mines

Wage/salary at entry level After six years of a service Beyond

(Entry level) Low	Minimum	Maximum
Lowest basic remuneration	High basic remuneration + notch	Highest basic remuneration + notch

This table above shows the disparities between the new recruits and those employees who have been serving the company for six years and above.

In this case, black employees do not get their salaries and wages adjusted. We have blacks who have been working for the mines for over thirty-six years and still paid on low entry-level remuneration. I have been working for the mines since 2001 and still get paid on low entry level.

Only white employees are getting their salaries adjusted. However, there will be less than 2% of whites who will be found eking out under the same treatment as given to blacks. There has been one union member I was with in the trade union leadership who wanted to challenge the disparities alluded to but was quickly harshly silenced by her rivals within the leadership. This comrade was expelled from the office of the union on baseless and falsified crime. She was then granted a stress leave by the employer as the matter was becoming volatile due to the fact that the highest office of the trade union had to intervene to resolve the matter. This matter was put to rest after she came back from leave, but she did not have any more strength to start all over from where she left. The only problem this comrade had was that she wanted to keep the fight against such unfairness for herself and did not want to share with us, her comrades, about the fact of the matter, which made her fail to win the battle. It could have been the reason that she wanted to hold the employer at ransom, but unfortunately, things did not go very well in her favour.

In this sector, corruption has reached a point where unionists tend to take advantage of companies not complying with South African laws and demand bribes from mine managers so the company will not get reported and exposed to the authorities for non compliance, ,This has happened so many times.

I want to assure the reader that this is the exact reflection of the wage and salary discrepancy in this sector. It is happening in front of the unions that are supposed to be protecting the rights of the workers. For those blacks sitting in the management offices, they just find themselves to be ordered to run around those offices like headless chickens. They are expected to be doing their jobs and also those of their underperforming white managers who have been promoted based on the skin colour. These blacks are made to think that in actuality they have been done a favour for them to be sitting in those offices. Hence they will return a favour by helping white officials on their jobs, and this has been a normal practise in this sector. Black managers will hardly associate themselves with blacks who are the lowest paid as they were made to think that they are no longer part of blacks but belong to the white society within the operational parameters and that has been made normal as well. Black people in mining were shaped up to run around like small boys and fight for positions like real men.

Now when you carefully read the reflection from above, you will notice that black, Indian, and coloured employees have been misrepresented and victimized on a serious note, where they were excluded from participating in wealth accumulation in mining.

In this phenomenon, a person would be very naïve to suggest that everything should be left unattended to, since from 1867 up to date, blacks have been excluded from participating in the riches of the earth of South Africa, which has benefited white society remarkably. And the South African media turn a blind eye on such irregularities today.

When the people of the country call upon the government to run the mines, it is simply because of the manner in which the wealth from mining has been distributed. It is unfortunate that the media started running around the world with this news and painted a very dark picture about nationalization. Had the investors been made aware of such atrocities surrounding our mines, they would have indeed tried to find another country to invest in. The most important thing is that South African media should stop lying to the world and start exposing what whites are doing to their black counterparts in this sector. We will not build a good country should we keep lying about the true reflections of the country as this will keep driving blacks and whites far apart from each other, which has been very destructive to our young democracy. We are gradually reaching a point where we should be saying this democracy is now old enough to be expected to have produced far better results.

White people still believe that blacks should stay as far as possible from the wealth of the country and only make noise in politics as this wealth belongs to them. This notion must be redressed. This type of a sentiment shows how ignorant and unappreciative most of the whites are in South Africa. Despite all the agony blacks have been put through in SA, they still had the tenacity to extend their hands to the white communities and say let's be friends and compatriots again. Whites misconstrue this and take it as a weakness. (I take into cognizance the fact that we do have some whites who have really shown remorse for bringing the dignity of blacks down to nothing and are ready to move on and give democracy its tall.) We must also salute white comrades who have been helping our freedom fighters to achieve liberation in South Africa. They really had a choice to support apartheid and benefit from it but decided to go down with the then oppressed natives. I hope their offspring benefit from the fruit-tree of the liberation, wherever they are.

Should South Africans support the motion of mines nationalization, our communities and workers across the colour in the sector will be fully represented for equitable wealth distribution as opposed to the current practice where only white minority and few corrupt political leaders are only ones benefiting from the wealth generated. , If you listen to South African news very carefully, all white people are the ones opposed to nationalization, and of course, including a few corrupt leaders who are engaging in our mines without being noticed and benefiting from this sector without disclosing, which would have been deemed as conflict of interest. South African media failed to report the true reflection of how blacks are being treated in this sector, the reason could be that either they do not know what is going wrong in the sector and yet they rush into criticising the sentiment of nationalizing mines or they are simply turning a blind eye as though they do not know of such atrocities alluded to by the author. The fact is, if the media is so keen on mining productivity, why are they not eager as well to know about the well-being of the mine workers?

If the government of SA had made a thorough investigation and known all the pros and cons in the actual operations of the mines, they would have been in for a great shock when they learnt how black people are ill-treated in this sector. Whoever is informing the government about the operations in this sector, have not been honest and transparent. You will never know that you do not know something until you have realized that you do not know them. In this regard our government must form a task team to find out about these, and later engage our media and let them report the true reflections of the atrocities in the mining sector.

The mining company which is known to the author has released this statement in 2002: The group housing policy which was ratified in May 2002 encourages and supports employees, where possible, to own homes where they are provided. (The name of the mining company has been withheld for legality purposes.)

The company further stated and released their employee statistics in their infrastructural document. This is what was captured,

Local employees	1995	2003	variance
	34%	43%	+9
Transitional employees	16%	42%	+26
Migrant employees	50%	15%	-35

According to the communication above, the organization suggested that they will assist and facilitate provision of basic infrastructure in certain existing informal settlement. They further argued that the group's sustainable habitat policy aims to ensure that housing and living conditions remain envisaged.

In actuality, when you truly drive around the communities in the area within which the mines operate, the conditions within the communities are so nightmarish.

Basically, should we finalize the ideology of nationalization or even state owned and proceed with the conversion of ownership to the government, all stake holders' representation will be envisaged in this sector – private representative, employee representative, government representative, and community representative. And this will be a strategic forum which would oversee wealth redistribution and the same forum would constitute a human resources development committee (HRD). In South Africa, private companies have a strong tendency to violate the laws of the country and get away with it.

Young People's Party in South Africa has successfully made a submission to the parliamentary portfolio committee on the establishment of state-owned mining company and also encouraged debates on the issue. The youth league made it unequivocal the fact that 15% of Africans are still living in poverty according to their research. They have further alluded to the fact that 18 million out of the 48 million people in the country are still trying to figure out as to what is the benefit of the so called freedom for them as they are still living in poverty-stricken communities. It will need true patriotism for one to care for the downtrodden youth league had indeed reflected the features of patriotism by supporting the idea of mine nationalization which will benefit all South African communities in the country. In their submission, the young made it clear that their expertise afforded them the knowledge to differentiate nationalization from the proposed establishment of the state-owned mining company.

In my view as a writer, should our government delay debates or unnecessarily prolong this debate on converting our mines in a possible partnership with the government, our government will find it very difficult to cope with mass protests and ever-growing poverty around the communities. Hence only a few people will remain the benefactors from the wealth of the mining. The notion that our media is suggesting by saying that this route will scare the investors away cannot be entertained as the investors' interests are based on the profitability of the operation and not the man behind the operation. To me this remark is an insult to the investors as it could be interpreted in such a manner which will give the impression that our investors will only invest in the country if our mines are left to benefit only whites in South Africa which is the problem we need to resolve in this call for nationalization.

I, therefore, strongly argue that the young people of the country have a responsibility to unfold a procedural fairness by opening a debate on mining nationalization and giving young people of the country a platform to have their say. I also envisage that the debate would not necessarily dwell on whether or not we should nationalize our mines but rather on how best the government could run the operations efficiently and profitably. This is what the investors are interested in and not in the manner in which the naïve media interprets.

The ANC has always been involved in policy reviews; there have been lengthy policy review processes in preparation for its conferences. The starting point for the policy review process was the existing policy positions adopted by the fiftieth national conference in December 1997 in Mafikeng. The 1997 conference confirmed that successful economic transformation required a set of economic policies that were mutually re-enforcing and which, as a package, addressed the structural problems in the economy. These were some of the objectives set out at the fiftieth general conference:

- A redistribution of wealth, income, and opportunities in favour of the poor and the historically disadvantaged
- A society in which sound health, education, and other services are available to all
- The popular involvement and participation of all South Africans in the economy and in economic decisions.

At this point in time, the ANC is preparing for its conference in 2012. The politics ahead of any party conference have their own set of dynamics with different factions, groupings, and individuals either seeking power or trying to retain their existing power base. Because the stakes can be high at times, things can get dirty. That is why we have witnessed some of the leaders being tried within the leadership. The period leading up to the ANC National Conference being held in 2012 has been characterized by what could only be described as some rough power games not unlike those seen on movies. Things have got rather personal at times with individuals being branded and labelled on both sides of the political spectrum. So, against this backdrop of political intrigue and infighting, what forces have been applied? Is there something sinister going on, or is this just normal politics where those in power want to retain their position and shares in mining? Or is it simply a case of career opportunism and the 'politics of the stomach' which creates fixation against mines nationalization?

The group is quick to question the faith of anyone who disagrees.

- Paranoia – any attempt to raise a different perspective is seen as part of conspiracy to overthrow the current leadership
- Personal abuse – vitriolic attacks and the deliberate spreading of malicious rumours have become a norm
- Regarding comrades with different views as opponents, the group typically tries to discredit other comrades by deliberately misconstruing their statements and publishing ridiculous and untrue versions of their arguments. It is without doubt that the majority of ANC leaders find these tactics very unpleasant. However, the influence of this group is on the rise.

The secretary general of COSATU, Mr Vavi, was recently furnished with an anonymous letter which contained death threats. This was heard on the news and confirmed by the COSATU deputy secretary. Mr Vavi had just publicly pronounced his opinion about the lifestyle audit which suggested that all the ministers, possibly including top political heads, should be audited. Could that be the reason why someone wants him eliminated?

We must salute the youth league for bringing about the debate on mine nationalization in spite of the vitriolic attack they are subjected to.

I personally give thumbs up to the few political heads. Indeed, you have the future of the young people of the country at heart. Blacks, whites, Indians, and coloured will indeed benefit from the possible conversion of our mines.

Abraham Mathebe
South Africa (Mineworker and NUM office bearer)
SA Mines

Second Part of the SA Mines Article

In the 2009 negotiator's conference comprising twenty-five unions in South Africa, trade unionists were afforded to raise questions and concerns in relation to South African economic sustainability.

Quoting from the *Bargaining Monitor*, Vol. 23, No. 171

One of the programmes in this conference was presented by Professor Steven Friedman. Steven Friedman is a research associate at the Institute for Democracy, director of the University of Johannesburg's Centre for the Study of Democracy.

In this gathering and during professor's presentation, one trade unionist asked the following question: How can you address the issue of poverty and unemployment when the government is still engaging in privatization?

Steven's response: Privatization is unlikely to be mentioned in the next few years. We are not living in that kind of environment at the moment. It is possible that a financial crisis gives people the space to say privatization has partly got us into this kind of mess.

In the article shared by *Business Report*, the National Union of Mineworkers (NUM) welcomed the idea of mines nationalization. Frans Baleni, who is secretary general of NUM, was being cited as the paper's source.

Baleni told the newspaper that mineral rights had already been nationalised under the African National Congress (ANC) government. Baleni further added that an audit of state mining activities, as well as a study of state entities that had mining rights, should be conducted to determine areas where greater state involvement could occur, and where they could be operational in the mining. Though we never had an official addressing of this matter within the NUM, I want to believe that the GS's comment will be welcomed by all in this union.

The world is still recovering from the recession, and when the imperialists could accept the failures of capitalism which made them cry a foul play in the dark of recession, we, indeed, should ask ourselves whether the time has not arrived for the government to take control of the key resources such as our mines and all other means of production coded in the mining charter.

The other factor that contributes to poverty is the manner in which *commission, conciliation, mediation, and arbitration* (CCMA) has been set to run the cases. The employer in this sector has been using the advantage of the miscarriage of the CCMA system against the mineworkers who are being dismissed in high numbers on illegitimate offences. This argument is wholly based on the following: When a case could not be resolved within the premises of the mine or in case a dismissal is given as a verdict, the case will be referred to CCMA. Should the applicant and the respondent fail to reach a consensus, a commissioner refers the case to the higher level which in this case will be arbitration. A dismissed worker will not be earning any salary or anything to sustain the family. This plight leaves a dismissed worker vulnerable without any remuneration. The employer has the prerogative to keep all the money of the dismissed, pending the hearing.

Should the parties fail to reach an agreement at this level, the case will therefore be referred to the labour court, which is where the nightmare starts.

Can you imagine a poor worker being dismissed and made to wait for a minimum period of three years before the case is heard at the labour court?

Many dismissed workers have been persuaded by commissioners to accept settlement, which is equivalent to a slap in a face as though they (commissioners) are getting bonuses for bringing two parties into an agreement for settlement. Due to the employer's arrogance, the CCMA cases drag until the dismissed decides to take any settlement offer from the respondent in order to avoid a deadly starvation in the family. About 90% of mine related cases have left most of black mineworkers downtrodden when the employer went back to the office victorious, undeservedly.

If the government of the ANC and their leaders do not consider all the facts alluded to since the beginning of this debate in South Africa that suggested the handing over of South African mines to NATIONALIZATION as opposed to PRIVATIZATION, history will, indeed, be negative on the ruling party. And the coming generations will spit on their graves for having disabled their parents from reaping what they have sown for decades as mineworkers who could have been advantageous to their offspring for their economic boost from childhood, Injustice thrives when a righteous keeps silent. In South Africa we need to be colour-blind and protect each other against the onslaught.

In a regional committee meeting of National Union of Mineworkers (NUM) held on the 06–07 March 2009 at Braamfontein in Johannesburg

There was a report informing the trade unionists captured in black and white deliberating that since the last year (referring to 2008) the leadership have been receiving notices and reports from their respective branches about the possible retrenchments in many companies. They further stated that many of their members have already lost their jobs, layoffs, and even their bonuses. They further reported that companies have a tendency to retrench workers and layoff some without following consultation processes, said the report. Workers were said to have been subjected to working for a week and be sent home at times with no wages paid out to them.

As this report was clearly captured, authentically speaking, over 90% of the affected workers will always be natives; the management of organisations will always insist that the company cannot lose skilled personnel by retaining unskilled labour during a financial-meltdown crisis, which in the professional running of a corporate makes sense. However, why are employees from previously disadvantaged communities always excluded from personal development programmes (PDP)?

In this case, management may argue this fact by only presenting few blacks included on PDPs, and when you look at the level of training recommended to these few, you will notice that it is at the level of semi-skilled as compared to their white counterparts who get trained to become foremen, artisans, engineers, metallurgists, and/or even plant managers.

I do not wish to waste any time in this note but would like to tell the reader how frustrating it is to the mineworkers to keep witnessing foul play where a specific racial group is prepared for and given opportunities to qualify for better positions in the mine when they are being marginalized as though they cannot adjust to the call responded to by a specific fortunate race. I really believe that privatization had been given an opportunity for decades to make difference in the lives of the people, but the only thing they have achieved remarkably has been nothing other than discrimination in profit making in a mining sector.

It has always been imperative for the government of South Africa to monitor how the wealth of mines has been distributed amongst the employees and to the surrounding communities as the mining charter insists rightfully so. The government should have noticed that monitoring the process with a remote control has failed dismally. This is about time for the government of the country to take over this sector and run it at the closer supervision other than assuming that things will get to normal. It has also come to my realization that the previous government officials led by the former president, Mr Mbeki, did not care at all about all these disparities encountered in this sector. Therefore, should the current president, Jacob Zuma, fail to honour this call and give it an intensive thought, he (Mr Zuma) could also be missing the tune of the masses of the country, calling enough is enough. I mean, how do you justify a dismissal of a mineworker who was subjected to a fabricated offence that is out of a company codification of offences? Yes the CCMA is there to rectify such irregularities but given the fact of the companies' financial muscles, most of the employees do not win such cases. If the company isn't happy with the finding, they simply refer the matter to the next level and it goes on and on. How far will a dismissed mineworker go without being able to provide food for the family?

I want to reiterate that the corrupt officials do not belong to the workers' trade unions; corrupt officials do not belong to our government either. Not any more should the people of the country put up with illicit conduct perpetuated by some of these leaders. If the people in mines have been previously drifting and detaching themselves from the so-called privatization in this sector, why can't they be listened to when they are ready to state all the reasons as to why they have always hated privatization?

We were supposed to be exhausting ideas on how best should the government run our mines and not wasting time on the whether-or-not issues as the concept of nationalization is long overdue. Given the background in this sector, only self-centred human beings will find the nationalization programme irrelevant.

The level of corruption, self-enrichment, and racial discrimination in the sector has reached a point where we say transformation is long overdue.

The following have always been commitments that flow from value embedded in the constitution of NUM, but for the NUM to succeed, we need a shared compact across all the divides in this trade union and across the nation.

- *Manyofonyofo arena go a amogela* (this is a Sotho term meaning, 'We will not tolerate corruption.')
- We will act forcefully against wastage
- We will insist on value for money for the billions that we spend
- We will clean up the procurement system and take strong action against those who feed selfishly.

These values should have empowered everyone respectively in the sectors represented by the NUM but the arrogance of the employers and corruptions they are feeding have always been a hindrance for such achievement.

Even under circumstances of adversity, strong leadership will give extraordinary results. Not everything is gloomy; we can celebrate remarkable and effective achievement even in poor rural villages. Major advances in transport infrastructure and community initiatives that contribute to food security and local job creation can be realized.

We have had so many reports on infant mortality in rural areas attributable to lack of transport to hospital and lack of primary health care infrastructure. Is that not cruelty to the well-being of our people? We cannot all afford to migrate and live in towns in order to access such facilities. In this case, broad-based economic and social development is about commitment. It needs hard work and initiative by a government that is fully resourceful. In a capitalist economy this will only benefit the investors and top management team as it has always been happening with the current operational style in a mining sector. Of course, corrupt political leaders are also benefiting from this miscarriage operational system.

The trade unions have been struggling to redress such imbalances in the mining sector. Can we really work together as a nation and share the social and development goals in this sector? The answer is *yes!* But this can be even more effective in mining run by our government. As South Africans, we will have views in the day-to-day running of the mines. All the citizens of the country across the colour spectrum will be fully represented in the HRD committees that will be overseeing all the challenges encountered and reported to for further investigations without officials operating in silos.

As a nation, we have invited the world to join us in a great festival of football. We have demonstrated that Africa is ready to host world-recognized events of any nature. Particularly, South Africa has successfully hosted a giant project called football world cup. Mr Sepp Blatter rated South Africa 9/10 in preparations made for the world cup. We, indeed, could have achieved 10/10 should we have had more funds generated from this sector in question, let alone all the basic infrastructures our communities have been lacking.

In response to the economic crisis the world is recovering from including South Africa, a coordinated response to the crisis and collective efforts to reform the global financial system have been initiated by leaders of the G20 economies of which South Africa is an active member. Huge injections of finances by our government would have been more assertive in credit restoration flows and rebuilding of investor confidence. However, the mining sector has been reported to be the most recuperating sector from the economic meltdown in South Africa. Hence the employers are still raising the economic crisis as an excuse during negotiations.

Under President Zuma's leadership, the entire cabinet has been united in their commitment to restrengthen and accelerate the pace of transformation of our economy even in the recent economic setbacks. However, they cannot afford to fail to understand the importance of the conversion of our mines into nationalization which will boost the government's strategic service delivery programmes to the people, by the people, and for the people of the country as opposed to the individuals, by the individuals, and for the individuals.

The financial crisis should have been an eye opener to our government in SA. The crisis should have been regarded as a call for a new blend of skills development and renewal of schools and colleges. There is nothing more important than education in building national consciousness and pride. If the free education at the higher learning institutes is envisaged in the country, indeed, the government will need more funds. In this case, how much more could be generated from this sector? I mean, in the company I work for, the employer has just confirmed during a productivity presentation session facilitated by an outsider that the company is making a turnover of over five million Rands an hour which in a manager's brief reflected that the company has spent less than R66 per treated ton compared to R67 per tonnage as forecasted. These millions are generated in a three shift operation and nine hours working schedule per employee [Day, Afternoon and Night Shift].

In striving towards meeting the needs of the people and our economy, the crisis should have unveiled our eyes and installed a challenge to construct a new deal for our young people, new opportunities for school-leavers, and a new partnership between work seekers and employers, and responsible leadership in public service delivery as opposed to self-enrichment processes witnessed in a sector in question. Of course, we still have a syndrome of self-enrichment in the government which requires a radical approach and the possible confrontations if needs be.

Initiating growth and improvement and financial regulations are the immediate challenges to our government that is still under-resourced as compared to the developed countries.

Nationalization of South African mines should be regarded as a legitimate and authentic approach to our own South African challenges. We must demand greater courage and humility from our international investors for a just and stable future.

Upside risks to SA's medium to long-term inflation outlook remains a concern, particularly through administered prices which continue to grow in double digits. South Africa should be in a position to bail the public out of such crisis by developing self-sustainable income generating projects within the communities around the country. The wealth generation emanating from the mining sector must sustain the mineworkers and their families including the surrounding communities.

South Africa's financial system can prove to be highly resilient during the global financial crisis; the government of South Africa would be in a position to respond convincingly towards crisis if the resources were managed properly including our mines being well-managed on behalf of the public while managing risks in a volatile manner.

These are reforms that will contribute to the maintenance of South Africa's attractiveness as an investment destination. South Africa's role of managing its funds and resources has a convincing reflection as a financial centre in Africa.

Education in our country has been a largest budget commitment. In 2009, it was over R140 billion as reported in one of our NUM RC meetings increasing to R185 billion by 2012–2013.

Now, how do we realize these without proper funding schemes? We, therefore, need to secure more resources for our government to generate enough funds in order to be proactively responsive and effective in the implementation part of the process.

Cooperation with the private sector particularly in mining has not been unequivocal due to the tendency of not disclosing the revenues accumulated in the sector. We have known of some giant organizations that had to face the might of the law because they were found to have exported their production without having declared them to the South African government.

In 2009, as recorded budget allocation has been to the amount of R1 billion to the housing grant programme, and R2.5 billion being proposed for municipal infrastructure and grants, the total expenditure on housing and community amenities was said to rise from R69 billion in 2009 to over R98 billion in 2012–2013. Transport was over R65 billion a year over the medium-term expenditure framework (MTEF), which included the completion of the Gautrain project.

The public and future leaders cannot stress enough the relevance of nationalization of South African mines given all the financial commitment our government should take upon its shoulders for the benefit of the ordinary people of South Africa.

In fighting crime, public order and safety accounts were R78 billion in 2009, recorded to be growing to over R100 billion in the next three years. The budget was said to provide for an additional 22,400 police personnel aimed at restrengthening detective services and crime intelligence. Indeed, I do not have to include these recordings in vain. It is basically for you as a reader to understand as to where my argument emanates from regarding the debate on nationalization.

Such goals referred to will influence and translate into many programmes and policies; there are tens of thousands of office-bearers and officials whose efforts contribute to our suggested conversion of the sector in order for the country to be able to run its domestic affairs and duties responsibly and equitably. The mining sector has been tainted by corruption, corrupt officials in our government, and trade unions wear the same garments for their own identities amongst themselves, while on the other side stand corrupt mining bosses waiting for the corrupt officials to shake hands together sharing gifts, wining, and dining in pleasing one another in a pervasive manner at the expense of the poorest of the poor.

In a true sense, we are called upon to make an effort to protect the values on which our young democracy is founded, which bears fruit of freedom and financial liberty across the country.

The following was a report presented to the RC for injuries sustained by mineworkers without being reported to the relevant government departments (the names of the organizations and victims are known to the author).

An accident occurred where one of the comrades had a serious injury when he fell through a ceiling at the training centre and suffered a severe spinal injury. Unfortunately, during the investigation of the injury the inspector of mines was not present. The comrade is confined to a wheel chair.

Another accident occurred during September where a cde was working overtime shift on a Sunday. Inspectors were also not called in during the investigation. It was also reported that an enquiry was not conducted because the cde did not want to give the company a statement about what happened in the absence of his union representative. Both of the mineworkers reported to have injured were working for the same organisation and are currently wheelchair bound.

The fact of the matter is that, in any accident that occurs in the mine, inspectors should be called in to study the nature of the incident, have it recorded in the file, and suggest the preventative measures after some careful evaluation of the nature of the case. It is, therefore, the responsibility of both the company and health-and-safety representatives to make sure that procedures are being well attended to. There should be intensive audit by the inspectors in all the mines where injuries and fatalities have been reported to have occurred.

About sixty-four years ago, the African mineworkers union, led by great leaders of the revolution struggle such as J. B. Marks, J. J. Majoro, and the likes of Thabo Mofutsanyane staged a historic strike. They led a strike of mineworkers whose names were not captured in the history of mines in SA. Their graves did not have identity. This massive labour action by black mineworkers in the Witwatersrand triggered a massive protest from both capitalists and the government. This fight was a contagious effort to take forward work of other comrades in 1931. It was, therefore, captured as 1946 Mineworkers Strike. Mineworkers were still fighting for equal treatment which has not been realized to this day.

Sol. Plaatjie, who was the first secretary of the African National Congress, described the lives of black mineworkers in 1914 thus: 'Two-hundred thousand African miners, day and night sacrifice their dear lives in the bowels of the earth ranging from 1,000 to 3,000 feet beneath the earth, also sacrificing their lungs to the rock dust which affects miners with diseases like pneumonia.'

On 12 August 1946, the African mineworkers of the Witwatersrand came out on strike in support of demand for higher wages-10 shillings a day. They continued the strike for a week in the face of the most savage police attack in which, according to the records, 1,248 workers were wounded and a large number killed. But officially only nine workers were reported as killed during the strike. Lawless police and army violence smashed the strike, leaving corpses and casualties lying all over. Resources of the racist state were mobilized on a war footing against the unarmed workers.

In the twelfth national congress (24–27 May 2006), when he was stepping down as NUM secretary general, Gwede Mantashe addressed the congress and further stated: The national union of mineworkers must remain relevant and influential in the political and economic debates within the current discourse. We must not be afraid to raise our views even if they are not popular at any particular point in time. This is what makes us different.

When comrade Mantashe was stepping down, as it was his last congress in the trade unionism, the vacant position was highly contested by other comrades within the leadership of NUM. Comrade Archie Palane, who was the national chief negotiator in a diamond mine for the mineworkers, became the most supported candidate of the congress and could have won many votes in this congress. The outgoing Gwede Mantashe announced to the congress that comrade Archie Palane could no longer contest for the position because he was not a member in good standing. Almost the entire house of delegates went wild with anger as they did not understand as to what that meant because Archie was a national office bearer whose achievement in a diamond mine was remarkable. However, Archie was said to be employed by the union and not the elected office bearer (means that he never worked for the mine before).

The constitution of the national union of mineworkers stated: *Only members who have served as office bearers at branch and regional level may be nominated and elected into the positions of national office bearers, and/or workers who have been members in good standing for an unbroken period of seven years maybe nominated and elected into all positions of a national office bearer.*

A chaotic protest against the exclusion of Archie Palane went wild and caused delays in the congress until ANC top officials were called in to calm the situation.

I just found this proper to be alluded to because the contribution of comrade Archie Palane in mining should not go unnoticed.

The fact is that mineworkers seek to be led by true leaders; true leaders are people who get elected as officials and forget about self-promotion and enrichment at the expense of the people. *But* as for this time, corruption is at its tallest in all sectors, especially in the mines. Unions are still straggling to establish employee share ownership schemes even today (ESOPS). This is the scheme that must monitor 26% percent of the profit made in mining and distribute it among the employees and the surrounding communities.

Comrade Gwede Mantashe's 2006 report to the congress suggested that the union was making a lot of progress in the area of work; he stated that the number of companies that have bought into the concept of ESOPS was growing. He further stated that the union had not developed sufficient capacity at the company level to take up this issue. They (the union) are battling to put together a team of trustees in the individual companies.

'In most instances, it is the union that is less prepared for the challenge,' said Mantashe.

He said that the emerging trend was for the companies to include ESOPS as a means to gain a mining licence, with clear intentions of collapsing the schemes later.

As Mantashe deliberated on the delay of electing trustees for these funds, as an author I find myself to be asking the following questions,
'Is it possible that these delays are attributable to the fact that it is money involved here?'
'Is it because everyone wants to lay a hand on this money that they do not know what to do?'
'Is it possible that some corrupt-minded officials caused the delays of the establishment of the schemes which does not exist even today?'
'Is it not overdue for the government to have intervened in this sector and served the people honestly and discreetly?'

The trade unions federation (COSATU) will need to support the mines nationalization in South Africa as it is the route desired by the working class.

When the majority of affiliates live from hand to mouth, COSATU will be under-resourced. Therefore, the affiliation fees from the trade unions will eventually be reviewed. In this case, the likelihood of increasing the 1% that mine employees are already contributing as the monthly subscription to their respective unions is emerging. Now, how do you adjust a subscription of the workers to a higher percentage when a worker is earning less than R1,800 a month?

When we were at the central bargaining council, trying to amalgamate the key demands of the workers including wage increment, one shop-steward asked the council that as they are still earning R1,700 at the mine he is working for, how then are they going to pay 30% of medical aid that has also been part of the key demands in that meeting. Our principal negotiators only suggested that they will shelf the issue of salary disparities for a special task team that is not yet into existence.

The South African National Civic Organization (SANCO) as the only national civic body in the country is failing to take up issues that are relevant to the communities. The problem has seemed to be the issue of leadership structures being weakened and dominated by councillors. SANCO was supposed to be representing the communities independently. The areas within which mines are operating, SANCO should have been vigilant and ensured that the communities are well taken care of.

SANCO is supposed to be formed by civil society whose roles were to mobilize the society at large to pave up their destiny. It should galvanise communities into an active society that is resistant to the supremacy of neo-liberalism and the dominance of capitalism within mining.

Since COSATU established anti-privatization programme that was very active around 1990s, SANCO was never seen involved in campaigns of the alliance partners. The argument that might emerge after this deliberation suggesting that SANCO was really involved will not really hold water because the history of anti-privatization movement does not know anything about SANCO being involved, other than COSATU having tried to pass the baton of the programme to SANCO, which did not make any difference.

SANCO should have taken into cognizance the implication of high unemployment and inflation around the communities and all other aspects that deteriorate the well-being of the communities and come with strategic programmes to restore buying power within the communities. We cannot fold our hands and turn a blind eye on the sector going wild to disadvantaging its workers by robbing Peter to pay Paul.

Just going a bit back into history, the company, Consolidated Goldfields, was founded by Cecil Rhodes and his associates in London in 1887, and in its long involvement in the world of South African mining, Goldfields viewed itself as an embodiment of Victorian values. The company owned the richest gold mines in the country and made massive profits from mines such as East and West Driefontein, Kloof, Doornfontein, Dee kraal, Lebanon, Ventersport, and Leeudoorn with over 60,000 black miners, who were exploited. This company was the largest British organisation in South Africa.

In this sector, the companies offer inadequate compensation to injured workers which might have been caused by miscarriage of Health and Safety Act in the country. Disciplinary procedures were only made to be fair in theory, routinely engaged in the unfair dismissal of workers. This cruelty is still perpetuated in most of our mines today. Black mineworkers are still being charged for damage to company properties with or without any reflection of negligence from a worker' side. We have had cases involving injured mineworkers where most of them were attributable to poor communication between helpers and supervisors or managers.

If a black mineworker was booked off sick by a doctor, the companies would send out some of their officials to spy on that particular employee as to whether they are sickly in bed or just sticking around the neighbourhood. Should they be found to be not in their home premises, they will be suspected for abusing the sick leave and get recommended for categorization. This will happen very often against black mineworkers.

The mining management are indeed like an occupying power working to impose their will upon poor mineworkers whose effort in productivity never get appreciated. Thousands of mineworkers are illiterate and still need more education about their worker's rights and the rights to their well-being. They are hundreds if not thousands of miles away from home. They survive through superstitions hoping that some ancestor is taking care of their loved ones while they are out trying to save money for their travelling only during festive seasons. They are yet too fearful to practice their rights which the unions are trying to educate them about.

From the time of engagement of a black worker in the sector to this very day, black workers suffer discrimination and only few literates try to seize their equal rights from the hands of the employers.

Mineworkers are still living in hostels that are still partly converted to family units. They have been complaining about poor hygiene; this problem has obviously taken firm grip in their hostels. Cockroaches and other insects seem to be the only once at liberty in their hostels enjoying freedom of movement.

The problem of non-compliance to employment equity act [EEA] is still a big problem in this sector, are the unions not doing enough to make certain that the companies comply? The answer is: YES! They are not doing enough so they may still benefit from corruption of bribery; in as long as the companies are still not complying the companies will keep paying corruption fees to these corrupt leaders. Employers have a tendency of refusing to release shop stewards that they know are of a high influence when sitting in interviews, and only allow supervisors to release shop stewards whose knowledge of the EEA is neither here nor there. In the process of an interview, a shop steward asked the panel as to where the EEA was. In response, the panel comprising white line managers pointed to a white male and said, 'This is EEA,' and the shop steward gave the proceeding a blessing to go on.

My experience in mining has taught me that mine employers do not respect the basic human rights of its employees. Unions are still pretty much regarded as subversive institutions. Many of the miners are simply frightened of consequences if they have joined the unions. Some white employees still believe that unions are only for blacks, especially those whites who do not have a historical background about the establishment of trade unionism in 1880 by white workers. Most black graduates in this sector are dominated by misconceptions that suggest that unions are only for uneducated black mineworkers. They will only revolve around the union offices if they find themselves to be in trouble with their bosses.

Mine bosses are making big profits in all mines whilst the wallets of the ordinary mineworker runs dry in a pay day; one might have expected better from the bosses coming from overseas.

South African government has the power and financial leverage to persuade a large number of other business corporations and mining industry in general to criticize apartheid that is still going on in the sector. What stops them from doing so? Pure selfishness!

We have got the government of the country . . . We are in forever now, declared Smuts in March 1907 in the aftermath of the general election that swept Louis Botha's 'het volk' (the people) to power in the Transvaal. He was speaking to Sir Richard Solomon in South central of Pretorial.

These were associates who dictated the 'what to's' and 'what not to's' of the wealth of mines in the country. Jan Christiaan Smuts was a South African statesman and military leader who in 1911 together with Luis Botha formed the South African Party (SAP).

The gap between whites and blacks is still huge in terms of benefits and the entire treatment n as far as equality is concerned. We are still having a serious problem at this point in time as though much had never been done in terms of all the protests and blood shares alluded to in trying to achieve workers rights.

Employers are still continuing with their imperialist behaviour towards mineworkers.

I really fail to understand why the unions are failing to seek the intervention of Black Management Forum to visit the mines and start an auditing process on EEA and all other non-compliant reports always sent to the regional councils (RC). The mining charter was adopted as the guiding document in addressing all these issues of transformation, and it was just made to be useless by such endless non-compliances (this could be the harshest remark ever uttered against this charter).

On 18 April 2010, Vergenog mineworkers reported to the RC that the workers went on strike on their outstanding issues such as *living-out allow* and Medical aid allowance

At the end of the legal strike, about six mineworkers were charged and went to hearing. When a verdict was given all the six workers were dismissed from work. Their case was taken to CCMA on the 11 June 2010.

In the year 2010, how do we still find workers being dismissed practicing their democratic rights against their employer?

We were not supposed to be blaming the apartheid system even at this time as though we do not have the guiding principles of the constitution in the country, and even as we are trying to move towards a diversified new South Africa that is non-racist and non-sexist.

If we are still faced with the resistance to equality, we will keep looking back to the damage still protruding as the legacy of the apartheid. The apartheid system has created a massive pool of cheap and unskilled labour in mining made up of mainly black working class men and women suffering in precisely the way Marx predicted as being a natural development of capitalism. Classical Marxist theory has it that society is divided into two classes, the working class (proletariat) and the ruling class (bourgeoisie), whilst this is broadly still the case; racism is still an ugly feature of our society.

The unions must lead anti-racism campaigns so that our society is rid of this obscene remnant of apartheid.

As the issue of nationalization still needs a strategic approach, we should not shy away from the current issues of exploitation even if those who seek compromise in accommodation of racism will feel offended.

There can be no doubt that the structures of the unions need streamlining. We cannot keep compromising the workers and chase personal enrichment. The unions would be more efficient, more effective, and more able to influence the ANC and the government as the employer in mining programmes benefiting both the employer and the employee. And of course, we would have a much greater chance of intervening effectively in the transformation of the state structures and the society. Compromise has indeed taken its toll between the employer and the unions, and this cannot be in the interest of the workers.

In the COSATU policy conference of 15–17 May 1997, the following declaration was pronounced and adopted by all the affiliates (just to mention the few).

Minimum Wage

- To campaign for minimum wage setting for the vulnerable and the less-organised sectors of the economy using bargained wage levels taking into account the existing inequities and disparity in incomes as well as the struggle for a living wage.
- To develop a strategy to organise the unorganised, in particular, farm workers.
- To urge the government to monitor and to punish those who disregard the agreed to minimum wages.

Public Houses

- To call for provision of housing on a rental and purchase basis.
- To campaign for the establishment of a housing parastatal to co-ordinate housing delivery and to raise funds.
- A 5% prescribed assets investment dedicated towards housing
- To explore the mechanism of introducing a levy period
- To campaign for the establishment of housing brigades in communities to help fast-track housing delivery
- To campaign against high interest rates which make it impossible for most people to afford housing.

This conference took place against the background of the government's adoption of Gear, its impact on social spending and failure to create jobs, the deadlock in negotiations over the basic condition of employment bill at National Economic Development and Labour Council (Nedlac), widespread poverty amongst the unemployed and the working poor, the diminishing role of the state in the productive sector of the economy, as well as provision of basic services in 1997.

The Leadership: The leadership has many dimensions. First, we need leadership that can set long-term vision to mobilise society. Secondly, leadership is required to ensure effective implementation of policy objectives. South Africa has many good policies that remain vision documents due to lack of implementation. For example, companies will give bonuses that are based on the management's discretion and eventually benefit white clerks, artisans, and managers when black workers get a quarter of what has been offered to white employees.

Nevertheless, the management keeps reiterating to the unions that a bonus has been paid out on the management's discretion, which will always discriminate blacks from getting a better incentive in as much as their white counterparts would. What is also required is a leadership that is bold enough to tackle the laggards and corruption. If the officials and politicians make out that they will always hide under comradeship at whatever cost, this creates a wicked enticement for officials and politicians. We may be content that the government has provided millions of houses, when those houses are of below par construction and are actually uninhabitable

If the ANC wants to have one million members and possibly above its expectations, the organization's programmes must be well captured for the benefit of the citizens of the country across the colour spectrum. The government of the ANC must break the element of racism tend to bring the citizens of the country under one roof on a continuous equitable treatment irrespective of the skin colour of a worker, sex, and culture.

I want to share with you as the reader the most famous freedom charter adopted in South Africa which South African human rights were based on.

This is the freedom charter as adopted at the congress of the people (African National Congress) on 26 June 1955, and the National Union of Mineworkers' fifth annual congress.

We, the people of South Africa, declare for all our country and the world to know:

That South Africa belongs to all who live in it, black and white, and that no government can justly claim authority unless it is based on the will of the people;

That our people have been robbed of their birthright to land, liberty, and peace by a form of government founded on injustice and inequalities.

That our country will never be prosperous or free until all our people live in brotherhood, enjoying equal rights and opportunities;

That only a democratic state, based on the will of the people, can secure to all their birthright without distinction of colour, race, sex, or belief.

And, therefore, we the people of South Africa, black and white together equals, countrymen and brothers, adopt this freedom charter. And we pledge ourselves to strive together, sparing neither our strength nor courage, until the democratic changes set out here have been won.

The People Shall Govern!

Every man and woman shall have the right to vote for and stand as a candidate for all bodies which make laws.

All the people shall be entitled to take part in the administration of the country.

The rights of the people shall be the same regardless of race, colour, or sex.

All bodies of minority rule, advisory boards, councils, and authorities shall be replaced by democratic organs of self-government.

All National Groups Shall have Equal Rights

There shall be equal status in the bodies of the state, in the courts, and in the schools for all national groups and races.

All national groups shall be protected by laws against insults to their race and national pride.

All people shall have equal rights to use their own languages, and to develop their own folk culture and customs.

The preaching and practice of national race or colour discrimination and contempt shall be a punishable crime.

All apartheid laws and practises shall be set aside.

The People Shall Share in the Country's Wealth

The national wealth of the country, the heritage of South Africa, shall be restored to the people. The mineral wealth beneath the soil, the banks and monopoly industry shall be transferred to the ownership of the people as a whole.

All other industries and trades shall be controlled to assist the well-being of the people.

All people shall have equal rights to trade where they choose, to manufacture and to enter all trades, crafts, and professions.

The Land Shall Be Shared Among Those Who Work It

Restriction of land ownership on a racial basis shall be ended, and all the land re-divided among those who work it, to banish famine and land hunger.

The state shall help the peasants who implements, seeds, tractors, and dams to save the soil and assists the tillers.

Freedom of movement shall be guaranteed to all who work on the land.

All shall have the right to occupy land wherever they choose.

People shall not be robbed of their cattle, and forced labour and farm prisons shall be abolished.

All Shall Be Equal Before the Law

No-one shall be imprisoned, deported or restricted without a fair trial.

No-one shall be condemned by order of any government officials. The courts shall be representative of all the people.

Imprisonment shall only be for serious crimes against people, and shall aim at re-education, not vengeance.

The police force and army shall be open to all on an equal basis; they shall be helpers and protectors of the people.

All laws which discriminate on grounds of race, colour, or belief shall be repealed.

All Shall Enjoy Equal Human Rights

The law shall guarantee to all their right to speak, to organise, to meet together, to publishing right, to preach, to worship, and to educate their children.

The privacy of the house from police raids shall be protected by law.

All shall be free to travel without restriction from countryside to town, from province to province, and from South Africa abroad.

Pass Laws, permits, and all other laws restricting these freedoms shall be abolished.

There Shall Be Work and Security

All who work shall be free to form trade unions, to elect their officers, and to make wage agreements with their employers.

The state shall recognise the right and duty of all to work and to draw full unemployment benefits.

Men and women of all races shall receive equal pay for equal work. There shall be a forty-hour working week, a national minimum wage, paid annual leave and sick leave for workers, and maternity leave on full pay for all working mothers.

Miners, domestic workers, farm workers and civil servants shall have the same rights as all others who work.

Child labour, compound labour, the tot system, and contract labour shall be abolished.

The Doors of Learning and Culture Shall Be Opened

The government shall discover, develop, and encourage national talent for the enhancement of our culture life.

All the culture treasures of mankind shall be opened to all, by free exchange of books, ideas, and contact with other lands.

The aim of education shall be to teach the youth to love their people and their culture, to honour human brotherhood, liberty, and peace.

Education shall be free, compulsory, universal, and equal for all children. Higher education and technical training shall be opened to all by means of state allowance and scholarship awarded on the basis of merit.

Adult illiteracy shall be ended by a mass state education plan.

Teachers shall have all the rights of other citizens.

The colour bar in cultural life, in sports, and in education shall be abolished.

There Shall Be Houses, Security, and Comfort

All people shall have the right to live where they choose, be decently housed and to bring up their families in comfort and security. Unused housing space shall be made available to the people. Rent and prices shall be lowered, food plentiful, and no one shall go hungry.

A preventative heath scheme shall be run by the state.

Free medical care and hospital treatment shall be provided for all, with special care for mothers and young children.

Slums shall be demolished and new suburbs built where all shall have transport, roads, lighting, playing fields, crèches, and social centres.

The aged, the orphans, the disabled, and the sick shall be cared for by the state.

Rest, leisure, and recreation shall be the right of all.

Fenced locations and ghettos shall be abolished and laws which break up families shall be repealed.

There Shall Be Peace and Friendship

South Africa shall be a fully independent state, which respects the rights and sovereignty of all nations.

CONCLUSION

- I wish to see people of South Africa,
- Sharing the wealth of this country together, being able to celebrate the achievement of this country as beneficiaries together
- Teaching their children to respect cultures, traditions, and the norms of other groups
- Being able to beat corruption and expose the lawbreakers in the country
- Being able to recognize each other as fellow South Africans and extend the gratitude to the visitors from other countries
- Encouraging social interaction amongst the offspring of all South Africans for better understanding of different cultures, traditions and norms.

www.ingramcontent.com/pod-product-compliance
Lightning Source LLC
Chambersburg PA
CBHW021905170526
45157CB00005B/1977